W9-BWF-414

979.8
STR

C.1

3488 0000 401005

Strudwick, Leslie
Alaska

DATE DUE	BC#34880000401005 $16.95
	BORROWER'S NAME

DATE DUE

979.8   BC#34880000401005 $16.95
STR   Strudwick, Leslie
C.1   Alaska

Morrill Math & Science Academy
Chicago Public Schools
6011 S. Rockwell St.
Chicago, IL 60629

ALASKA

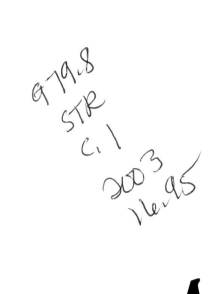

Leslie Strudwick

Published by Weigl Publishers Inc.
123 South Broad Street, Box 227
Mankato, MN 56002
USA
Web site: http://www.weigl.com

Library of Congress Cataloging-in-Publication Data available upon request from the publisher. Fax: (507) 388-2746 for the attention of the Publishing Records Department.

ISBN 1-930954-75-1

Printed in the United States of America
1 2 3 4 5 6 7 8 9 10   05 04 03 02 01

Project Coordinators
Rennay Craats
Jennifer Nault
Substantive Editor
Janice Parker
Copy Editors
Heather Kissock
Michael Lowry
Designers
Warren Clark
Terry Paulhus
Photo Researchers
Julie Pearson
Mark Bizek

Photograph Credits
Every reasonable effort has been made to trace ownership and to obtain permission to reprint copyright material. The publishers would be pleased to have any errors or omissions brought to their attention so that they may be corrected in subsequent printings.

All photos provided by Clark James Mishler unless otherwise noted.

Cover: Clark James Mishler; **Corel Corporation:** pages 6, 25; **Flavin Photography:** 13 (Frank Flavin); **Alaska Purchase Centennial Commission – Alaska State Library:** 17, 18, 19, 21.

CONTENTS

INTRODUCTION

Alaska is the most northerly state in the United States. It has a cold climate, rough land, open **tundra**, and few inhabitants. Alaska is known as "The Land of the Midnight Sun" because it experiences nearly continuous sun in the summer. In the winter, the state's northern region stays dark almost around the clock. During these times, the sun appears to never set, or never rise.

Alaska's land forms the largest peninsula in the Western Hemisphere. An entire country, Canada, separates Alaska from the United States mainland.

QUICK FACTS

The motto of Alaska is "North to the Future."

The state bird is the willow ptarmigan. It is a small arctic bird that lives on the tundra.

The Sitka spruce was named the state tree in 1962. It can be found throughout the central and southeastern parts of the state.

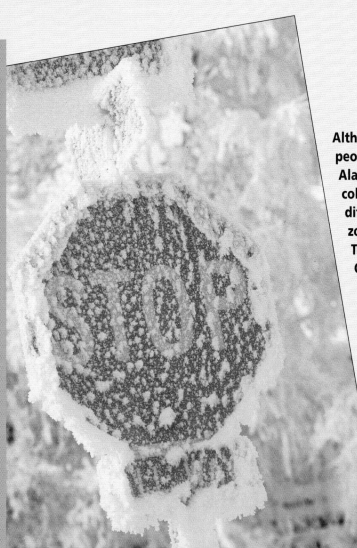

Although many people think that Alaska is always cold, it has four different climatic zones: Maritime, Transitional, Continental, and Arctic.

Getting There

Alaska is a **remote** state. Getting to it or traveling around it is not always easy. Visitors must drive through Canada or fly in. Once in Alaska, there are roads leading to some, but not all, of the major centers. The capital city, Juneau, can only be reached by boat or plane. There are no roads leading into or out of Juneau. This is true of many of the smaller cities and towns. The largest city in the state, Anchorage, has all the **amenities** of a large city: planes, trains, roads, museums, and shopping.

Seaplanes equipped with **pontoons** are known as floatplanes. Floatplanes are often the only way people get into and out of Alaska's remote regions.

QUICK FACTS

The state flag shows the Big Dipper **constellation** and the North Star. The Big Dipper, also known as the Great Bear, stands for strength.

The design of the state flag was drawn up in 1926 by a 13-year-old boy named Bennie Benson. He lived in Cognac, Alaska.

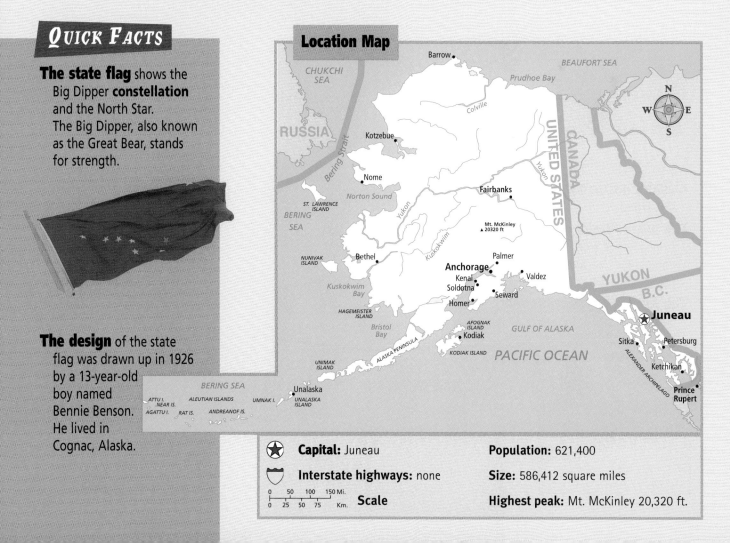

Location Map

CHUKCHI SEA

BEAUFORT SEA

Barrow

Prudhoe Bay

Colville

RUSSIA

Kotzebue

Bering Strait

Nome

Norton Sound

ST. LAWRENCE ISLAND

BERING SEA

Yukon

Fairbanks

UNITED STATES

CANADA

Mt. McKinley ▲ 20320 ft

NUNIVAK ISLAND

Bethel

Kuskokwim

Palmer

Anchorage
Kenai
Soldotna
Homer
Seward
Valdez

Kuskokwim Bay

HAGEMEISTER ISLAND

Bristol Bay

AFOGNAK ISLAND

Kodiak

GULF OF ALASKA

YUKON

B.C.

★**Juneau**

Sitka
Petersburg

ALEXANDER ARCHIPELAGO

Ketchikan

KODIAK ISLAND

PACIFIC OCEAN

UNIMAK ISLAND

ALASKA PENINSULA

BERING SEA

ATTU I.
NEAR IS.
AGATTU I.   RAT IS.   ANDREANOF IS.
ALEUTIAN ISLANDS   UMNAK I.

Unalaska
UNALASKA ISLAND

N
W E
S

★ **Capital:** Juneau

Interstate highways: none

0 50 100 150 Mi.
0 25 50 75 Km.
Scale

Population: 621,400

Size: 586,412 square miles

Highest peak: Mt. McKinley 20,320 ft.

Despite its distance from the United States mainland, Alaska's fascinating character and history contribute greatly to the nation. The land was bought from Russia decades before it became the forty-ninth state in 1959. Miners from the mainland traveled to Alaska in search of gold in the nineteenth century. Many settlers fell in love with the wilderness and chose to stay. These new settlers lived among the Inuit, who had been living in the region for thousands of years.

Alaska's immense rain forest contains trees that are hundreds of feet tall and up to a thousand years old.

QUICK FACTS

Alaska's nickname is "The Last Frontier."

The name Alaska comes from a Native word meaning "great land" or "that which the sea breaks against."

The Alaska Highway was designed to deliver military supplies during World War II.

QUICK FACTS

The giant king salmon is the state fish. It weighs up to 100 pounds.

Alaska's state flower is the forget-me-not. This flower grows throughout the state.

Tourists visit Alaska to enjoy all the outdoor beauty it has to offer. This includes hiking in the mountains, sailing past **glaciers**, and enjoying the dazzling northern lights. Alaska also attracts adventure seekers who glide over the icy tundra in dogsleds.

Among Alaska's many mountains is the tallest mountain in North America. Mount McKinley attracts expert mountain climbers to scale its 20,320 feet of snowfield-covered rock.

Every spring, king salmon swim upstream to spawn. Adult salmon will swim as far as 2000 miles.

Ice fields are composed of brittle, compacted snow with many deep crevices.

LAND AND CLIMATE

Alaska is the biggest state in the United States. From north to south, it is 1,400 miles long, and from east to west, it is 2,400 miles wide. The land varies from flat, bush-covered areas to mountain ranges.

The Alaskan landscape makes up for the sometimes less than pleasant climate. Alaska boasts the tallest mountain in North America, the largest number of glaciers, and the largest national parks in the United States.

The temperatures in the south are quite mild during summer months. The west, which borders the ocean, receives more rain and snow and is often cooler than the rest of the state. In the north, temperatures can hover near the freezing point in July. However, the majority of people living in and visiting Alaska are in the south and center regions of the state. They may experience −40 °Fahrenheit temperatures in the winter, but they enjoy summer temperatures of around 55 °F.

QUICK FACTS

Alaska is so large and has so few people living there, each person could have almost one square mile to him- or herself.

The highest temperature ever recorded in Alaska was 100 °F at Fort Yukon on June 27, 1915. The lowest was −80 °F at Prospect Creek Camp on January 23, 1971.

Alaska has rocky islands, a sandy coastline, thick forests, icy glaciers, and bare tundra. The state even has some active volcanoes!

Alaska's land and climate make it one of the most majestic places in the world.

At the Fort Knox Gold Mine, workers pour millions of dollars worth of gold.

NATURAL RESOURCES

Alaska is rich in natural resources. There are fish in the water, trees covering the land, and minerals in the ground.

Gold was the resource that started it all. Gold was first discovered in Alaska in 1880. Before this time, there had been few explorers and settlers in the area. Thousands of settlers came to the area in search of gold. Gold mining still exists today, but it does not employ as many workers as before. There are also mines for coal, silver, and zinc.

Alaska's two main **exports** are timber and fish. In fact, the state is the nation's top exporter of fish. Salmon is the most **abundant** catch. Halibut, herring, and shellfish, such as crab, earn top dollars for fishers as well.

Oil and gas are other key natural resources in the state. Almost 90 percent of the money earned by the state comes from the oil and gas industry. The huge Trans-Alaska Pipeline transports most of the oil produced in the state.

An average male Alaskan king crab will have a leg span of approximately 3 feet.

PLANTS AND ANIMALS

There is plenty of animal life in the Alaskan sky, on its land, and in its water. Thousands of bald eagles flock to the Chilkat River in the southeast each winter to feast on salmon. The eagle is the largest species of bird in Alaska, but it is not the only bird species. More than 400 different bird species live in the state.

Bears are another common sight. Grizzlies, black bears, polar bears, and a rare bear called the glacier, or blue bear, make their home in Alaska. Glacier bears are actually black bears that have a blend of gray and black hair, giving them a bluish hue. Visitors can also be on the look-out for caribou, deer, elk, fox, moose, mountain sheep, beaver, and lynx.

Alaska's waters are home to many fish and marine mammals. Fifteen different kinds of whale have been seen off Alaska's coast. Some of the most common are the gray whale, beluga whale, humpback whale, killer whale, and narwhal. Other sea animals include otters and seals.

Moose are the largest member of the deer family. Like other members of the deer family, their antlers are shed and regrown annually.

QUICK FACTS

There are more bald eagles in Alaska than in all other states combined.

Alaska is home to far more animals than people.

The Pribilof Islands of Alaska are home to the world's largest colony of seals. More than 1 million seals live on these islands.

From forest to marsh, Alaska has a variety of plant life. Among Alaska's plant life are bushes that produce juicy berries. Wild berries are everywhere, and they help keep many animals fed. The most common berry is the lowbush cranberry. Just a few of the many wild berries to be enjoyed are strawberries, blueberries, and cloudberries.

Its small human population and untouched wilderness areas keep Alaska's environment **pristine** and healthy. Compared to many places, the air and water are very clean. Plants and animals that have been in Alaska for thousands of years continue to exist. As more people move to Alaska, some of these plants and animals may become threatened.

The town of Sitka is surrounded by many local wildflowers.

Skagway's Klondike Gold Rush National Historic Park attracts many tourists.

TOURISM

Tourism in Alaska has grown over the last few decades and continues to grow each year. With so many places to visit, it is easy to see why Alaska has gained in popularity. The majority of visitors are from the United States—close to 80 percent. The most popular months for tourists to enjoy Alaska are June, July, and August.

Cruise ships that sail up Canada's coast and along Alaska's southern islands are very popular. A favorite part of these trips is Glacier Bay, where tourists admire the beautiful ice forms.

Some of the most visited places in the state include Portage Glacier, Mount McKinley, Skagway's historical gold rush district, and the Anchorage Museum of History and Art. The Ketchikan Totems and Sitka's Russian Church and Dancers also draw large numbers of tourists.

The Archangel Dancers represent a part of Alaska's colorful Russian history.

The Tongass and Chugach National Forests contain most of Alaska's timber resources.

INDUSTRY

The first major industry in Alaska was the fur trade. Russian explorers took furs back to Russia to sell. Fur trapping still exists in Alaska, but on a much smaller scale.

The gold industry brought the next big flow of money into the state. This was followed by the oil and gas industry in the 1970s. A large oil and gas **reservoir** was found near Prudhoe Bay in 1968. Geologists guessed that it was twice as large as any other oil field in North America at the time. Seven oil companies joined together and built the Trans-Alaska Pipeline.

The $9 billion pipeline is 800 miles long. Because of its size, the pipeline is one of the top tourist attractions in the state.

Tourism is the latest industry to boom in Alaska. Along with service and government jobs, tourism, timber, and fishing are the top industries in the state today.

QUICK FACTS

From 1969 to 1977, 70,000 people were involved in building the Trans-Alaska Pipeline. The pipeline runs from Prudhoe Bay to the port of Valdez.

One of the largest oil spills happened off the Alaska coast. A super **tanker** called the *Exxon Valdez* spilled 11 million gallons of oil into Prince William Sound.

The 800-mile Trans-Alaska Pipeline is underground for about half its length. The other 400 miles of pipeline are aboveground, held up by supports.

GOODS AND SERVICES

Few goods and services can be found outside the major centers in Alaska. The best place for people to find what they need is in Alaska's capital, Anchorage. Most of these goods have been flown into the city from elsewhere in the country. Anchorage has the largest airport in the state. It also handles more **cargo** than any other airport in the United States. Some Alaskans are dependent on air travel for the distribution of goods because not all areas have roads or railroads. In fact, one out of every fifty-eight Alaskans is a registered pilot.

All the conveniences of modern life can be found at the Anchorage Mall.

QUICK FACTS

Much of Alaska's employment is **seasonal**. During summer, the unemployment rate is much lower than it is in winter.

Rural communities in Alaska usually have a higher unemployment rate than urban centers.

Only three states in the nation have fewer roads than Alaska: Rhode Island, Delaware, and Hawaii.

The cost of living is high in Alaska because so many goods and materials have to be brought into the state. Providing services and medical care to remote areas in Alaska is expensive. Also, the cost of goods is high because there is little or no competition. In smaller centers such as Stebbins, food can cost up to 130 percent more than in other cities in the United States.

Four of the top ten most expensive cities in America to live in are found in Alaska. These cities are Anchorage, Fairbanks, Juneau, and Kodiak.

The government is a large employer in Alaska. Nearly 24 percent of Alaskans work for the federal, state, or local governments.

Although the cost of living is high, so are most of the salaries people earn. By charging more for their services, Alaskans can offset the high cost of living.

Within forty-eight hours of being caught, an Alaskan salmon can find its way onto the plates of diners in Paris or Tokyo.

Alaskan crabs fetch high prices from consumers.

Blanket tossing is an activity in which hunters are tossed into the air for whale-spotting purposes.

QUICK FACTS

The Aleutian Islands are named after the Aleut.

When the ocean is frozen, people can walk from Alaska to eastern Russia.

The totem poles found in Alaska are made by the Northwest Coast Natives.

FIRST NATIONS

The First Nations peoples had been living in Alaska for thousands of years before the arrival of Russian explorers. Some scientists think that the First Nations peoples came to North America from Asia as early as 12,000 years ago. At that time, a **landbridge** joined western Alaska to eastern Russia. First Nations peoples are thought to have followed food sources such as the woolly mammoth across this landbridge.

First Nations groups have their own beliefs about their origins. These beliefs explain how the land was created and how they came to live on it.

Today, there are four separate First Nations groups in Alaska. They are the Aleuts, Athabascans, Inuit, and the Northwest Coast Natives, which include the Tlingit, Haida, and Tsimshian. The cultures of these peoples are still rich and alive in Alaska. While many live modern lives, others prefer traditional ways of living. Many still hunt, fish, and make tools and crafts.

In 1998, a group of Haida people made a ceremonial canoe trip from Masset, British Columbia, to Juneau. They traveled over 300 miles by canoe.

Alaska prospered during the gold rush, and new communities and businesses developed to meet the gold seekers' needs.

EXPLORERS AND MISSIONARIES

Vitrus Bering was hired by Peter the Great of Russia to explore the North Pacific Ocean. In 1741, he came upon what is now Alaska. This was the first of many Russian voyages to the area in search of fur. Bering died soon after his discovery and was buried on an island off the Alaskan coast. The island was named Bering Island after him.

In 1784, the first permanent settlement was built on Kodiak Island. From there, Aleksandr Baranov controlled the trapping and trading posts on the mainland. Although Russians controlled Alaska during the late 1700s, other explorers traveled the area, including James Cook, George Vancouver, and Juan Perez.

QUICK FACTS

Vitrus Bering, who explored Alaska on behalf of Russia, was not from Russia, but Denmark.

Grigori Shelekhov founded the first Russian settlement on Kodiak Island.

Cook Inlet and Mount Cook are both named after the early explorer Captain James Cook.

BRACKETT'S TRADING POST.

Trading posts supplied gold prospectors with the essentials they needed for survival.

EARLY SETTLERS

In the mid-1800s, Russia's interest in Alaska **declined** because it was not seeing enough of a profit to make having the colony worthwhile. Russia offered to sell the land to the United States. The United States Secretary of State, William Seward, decided to offer the Russian government $7.2 million for the region. At less than 2 cents an acre, the United States bought the land in 1867.

Seward received some criticism for the purchase. Those who thought Alaska had little to offer referred to the deal as "Seward's Folly" or "Seward's Mistake." This mistake was quickly forgiven with the discovery of gold near Sitka in 1880.

William Seward

QUICK FACTS

In 1912, Alaska earned territorial status within the United States.

Industries developed as the population grew. The first salmon canneries were built in Klawock and Old Sitka in 1872.

After gold was discovered, many settlers came to the area. People moved to Alaska in droves hoping to find the biggest gold **nugget**. The largest gold deposits were found near Nome, Juneau, and Fairbanks.

Many of the early settlers were not prepared for Alaska's cold climate. Those who came unprepared faced starvation and exposure to freezing temperatures. Settlers came so quickly that there were few government laws to control the **masses**. Alaska was known as the "Wild North."

Gold discoveries were made in the neighboring Yukon Territory as well. Traffic through Alaska increased as prospectors made their way to Canada. Settlements grew into communities with churches, newspapers, and other services. In 1900, Juneau replaced Sitka as Alaska's capital. That same year, Alaska adopted a code of laws and a court system.

QUICK FACTS

The Hudson's Bay Company founded Fort Yukon in 1847.

A year after the United States bought Alaska, the U.S. Army was sent to keep control of the area.

In 1891, the first oil claims were made in Cook Inlet.

During the Alaskan gold rushes, many prospectors returned home with small fortunes.

POPULATION

Although Alaska's population is small, it has steadily increased since the early 1980s. At that time, there were close to 400,000 people living in the entire state. Today, there are slightly more than 620,000 people living in the state. About 260,000 people live in the state's largest city, Anchorage. Fairbanks is the next largest city, with about 85,000 people. The capital city, Juneau, has only 31,000 people. It is the third largest city in the state.

Most Alaskans are either from the United States and Canada, or they are of Russian **descent**. Native Americans account for about 16 percent of Alaska's population. Most are Inuit or Aleut. While some Native Americans live in cities, most live in smaller towns and villages.

Other groups that make up Alaska's population include Hispanics, African Americans, and Asians, including Filipinos, Koreans, and Japanese. Most of these groups live in Alaska's urban centers.

Over 30 percent of Alaska's population is under the age of eighteen.

QUICK FACTS

African Americans make up about 4 percent of Alaska's population.

Some Native Americans in Alaska use fur fans in dance ceremonies.

The Alaska State Capitol was completed on February 2, 1931.

POLITICS AND GOVERNMENT

Like each state in the Union, Alaska is governed on local, state, and federal levels. The state has a governor and a lieutenant governor who are each elected to four-year terms. The governor **appoints** the head of each of the fourteen state departments. The Senate and House of Representatives make up the Alaskan legislature. Forty representatives are elected to the House every two years. Twenty senators are elected every four years. Local government is not divided into counties as in other states. Instead, the state is divided into cities and **boroughs**.

QUICK FACTS

On January 3, 1959, Alaska became the second-last state to join the United States. The only state to join the United States after Alaska was Hawaii.

Alaska is represented in the United States Congress by two senators and one representative.

The first state legislature sat in Juneau in 1959.

In 1971, Congress approved the Alaska Native Claims Settlement Act. This act granted 40 million acres of land and $900 million to Alaska's Native Americans.

The Federal Office Building is in Juneau.

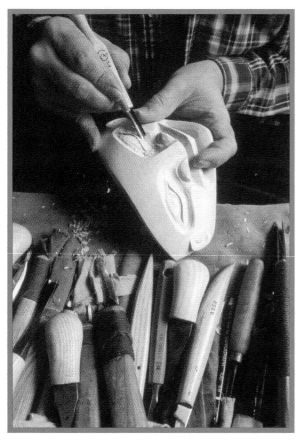

CULTURAL GROUPS

Native Americans make up the largest minority group within Alaska. Long before Russians or other explorers first traveled to the region, the First Nations peoples had their own rich culture. They had their own belief system, ceremonies, and arts and crafts. They used the resources available to them for practical and ceremonial purposes. For example, they carved ivory from walrus tusks to make harpoon heads and knife handles. They also carved dolls and sculptures from it. Jade and **soapstone** are other materials used in Native American carvings. Many of the ancient art and craft traditions among Alaska's Native Americans continue today.

QUICK FACTS

Igloo means "snowhouse."

Animals important to the Northwest Coast Natives are shown on their totems. Totems often feature eagles, whales, wolves, bears, ravens, beavers, and frogs.

The First Nations peoples of Alaska used copper as a sign of wealth. Copper plaques were **etched** and shaped into shields. "Coppers" were given names and histories, and were considered very powerful.

Many people who live in Gambell hunt marine mammals for food.

The Northwest Coast Natives that live in the southeastern part of the state continue to build totem poles. Totem poles are carved from huge cedar trees. They record the history, culture, and life events of the people who carve them. Totem poles include symbols for **ancestors** or **clans**. They are painted with vegetable or mineral dyes.

Usually, when people think of living in Alaska, igloos come to mind. Very few people, if any, live in igloos anymore. However, igloos are still used by Inuit hunters out on the frozen ocean or tundra. They are built as temporary shelters for the period of the hunt.

Totem poles still play an important role in the lives of some Alaskan people.

QUICK FACTS

Some traditional foods of Alaskan Native Americans are meat, fish, and berries.

Beadwork is a common craft among Native American women.

The Aleut are known for their excellent basket weaving.

The expression "low man on the totem pole" is misleading. The bottom ten feet of a totem pole are usually carved by a master carver, while **apprentices** complete the rest. The characters at the bottom of the totem pole are usually the most significant.

ARTS AND ENTERTAINMENT

Although the northern lights are not an art form, they could be. Also called *aurora borealis*, these dancing lights might provide one of the best forms of entertainment within the state. Northern lights are naturally occuring colored lights in the upper atmosphere. They are most visible near Earth's magnetic poles. Fairbanks is considered one of the best places in the world to see the northern lights.

To immerse yourself in Alaskan culture, Anchorage is the place to visit. It has art galleries, museums, theaters, a symphony orchestra, and an opera house. The Anchorage Historical and Fine Arts Museum houses an art gallery showing works of art from Alaska and around the world. The museum also has displays artifacts from First Nations cultures.

QUICK FACTS

Fairbanks celebrates Golden Days in late July. This event honors the discovery of gold with parades, parties, and sports.

Nome holds an annual polar bear swim in May. The brave (or crazy) participants jump into the freezing Bering Sea.

The Heritage Library Museum in Anchorage features Native American artwork, including tools, paintings, costumes, and beadwork. Anchorage has the largest museums, but many other great museums can be found across the state.

There are many festivals, fairs, and celebrations throughout the year. Many festivals occur during summer months, when the sun shines almost around the clock. Most towns have activities to celebrate the **summer solstice**.

The World Eskimo-Indian Olympics were founded in Fairbanks in 1961. High kicking, blanket tossing, and drumming are just a few of the events held there.

Carvings of animals were traditionally given as toys to children.

QUICK FACTS

Alaska celebrates Oktoberfest in the fall.

Inuit ice cream is a popular treat across Alaska. Traditionally, it is made from whipped berries, seal oil, and freshly fallen snow.

Traditional carvings made from sea mammal ivory are still made by Native Americans in Alaska.

Jade is a traditional gemstone used in carving. The stone comes in many colors: green, black, yellow, brown, white, and red.

SPORTS

One of the most popular sports in Alaska is dog mushing, or dogsled racing. In fact, it is Alaska's official state sport. Hundreds of races are held every year, from local matches to world championships. There are different kinds of races, from sprint mushing to long-distance racing. Winners of sprint races are determined by speed, over distances of 12 to 15 miles. Long-distance races can take many days, even weeks, as the racers travel great distances.

The Iditarod Trail Sled Dog Race is one of the oldest races run in Alaska. Since its beginning in 1973, the Iditarod has been lengthened several times. It is now about 1,100 miles long. The race starts in Anchorage and goes up and across the state, ending in Nome. Today, winners often take about nine days to finish the course.

QUICK FACTS

The first woman to win the Iditarod was Libby Riddles in 1985. It took her eighteen days. Susan Butcher then won it for the next three years in a row.

The size of a dogsled team usually ranges from seven to twenty dogs on a single team.

Winners of the Iditarod have won up to $350,000.

The Iditarod is nicknamed the "Last Great Race on Earth."

Other popular sports in Alaska are skiing, kayaking, and baseball.

The World Eskimo-Indian Olympics begin with a race called the Race of the Torch. The race winner lights the Olympic torch that year.

For three days in mid-July, Native peoples from Alaska, the Pacific Northwest, and Canada gather in Fairbanks for the World Eskimo-Indian Olympics. Traditional Alaskan competitions are held, including ear-pulling, fish cutting, knuckle hopping, and high kicking.

For nature lovers, kayaking, country skiing, and white water rafting are a great way see the state.

In the town of Ketchikan, kayakers paddle along historic Creek Street.

White water rafting is a great way to see Alaska's magnificent countryside.

Brain Teasers

1

Mount McKinley is the highest peak in North America. How high is it?

Answer: At its highest point, Mount McKinley is 20,320 feet above sea level.

2

Many of the highest mountains in the United States are in Alaska. How many are there?

Answer: Seventeen out of the twenty highest peaks in the United States are in Alaska.

How was the Valley of Ten Thousand Smokes created?

4

Answer: Alaska has almost seventy volcanoes. Some of these have erupted in the past century. In 1912, Novarupta Volcano erupted, creating the Valley of Ten Thousand Smokes. This is now part of Katmai National Park and a popular tourist attraction.

3

What is Mount McKinley's other name?

Answer: Mount McKinley is also known by its Native name—Denali. Denali is an Athabascan word meaning "high one."

5

How many lakes does Alaska have?

Answer: There are more than three million lakes. There are also more than 3,000 rivers.

6

Alaska is host to the largest gathering of bald eagles in the world. Where is it?

Answer: More than 3,500 bald eagles gather along the Chilkat River each year to feast on salmon.

7

Is it possible to experience an earthquake in Alaska?

Answer: Yes, Alaska has approximately 5,000 earthquakes every year. Most of these are so small they cannot even be felt. However, of the ten strongest earthquakes ever recorded, three were in Alaska.

8

What is the only U.S. capital that cannot be accessed by road?

Answer: Juneau is the only capital city in the United States that can only be reached by boat or airplane. There are no roads leading into or out of Juneau.

FOR MORE INFORMATION

Books

Alaska Almanac: *Facts About Alaska.* Anchorage: Alaska Northwest Books, 1996.

Brown, Tricia. *Children of the Midnight Sun.* Anchorage: Alaska Northwest Books, 1998.

Cohen, Daniel. *The Alaska Purchase.* Brookfield, CN: Millbrook Press, 1996.

Seibert, Patricia. *Mush!* Brookfield, CN: Millbrook Press, 1992.

Stefoff, Rebecca. *Alaska.* New York: Benchmark Books, 1998.

Wadsworth, Ginger. *Susan Butcher, Sled Dog Racer.* Minneapolis: Lerner Publications, 1994.

Walsh Shepherd, Donna. *Alaska.* New York: Children's Press, 1999.

Web Sites

You can also go online and have a look at the following Web sites:

The State of Alaska
http://www.state.ak.us

The US 50: Alaska
http://www.theus50.com/alaska

Fact Monster: Alaska
http://www.factmonster.com/ipka/A0108178.html

Alaska Tourism Development
http://www.dced.state.ak.us/tourism

I Love Alaska
http://www.ilovealaska.com

Some Web sites stay current longer than others. To find other Alaskan Web sites, enter search terms such as "Alaska," "Anchorage," "Iditarod," or any other topic you want to research.

GLOSSARY

abundant: a large amount

amenities: services and features that help make living convenient

ancestors: ancient relatives

appoint: to name or sign officially, often used within the government

apprentices: people who learn by working under the guidance of a skilled master

boroughs: living areas within a city

cargo: goods transported by ships and airplanes

clans: groups of families

constellation: any group of stars that have been given a name

declined: decreased

descent: one's family background, including distant relatives

etched: engraved

exports: shipments to other countries

glaciers: large, slow-moving blocks of ice

high kicking: an Inuit sporting activity where competitors jump up and kick a hanging object

landbridge: a strip of land that connects two continents

masses: large groups of people

nugget: a lump of precious metal

pontoons: floating devices attached to seaplanes

pristine: a natural and undeveloped state

prospectors: individuals who search for precious metals such as gold

remote: far away

reservoir: an underground pool

seasonal: dependent on the time of year

soapstone: a soft, oily stone used for carving

spawn: to give birth

summer solstice: the beginning of summer in the Northern Hemisphere

tanker: a large ship designed to transport liquid, especially oil

tundra: large, treeless plains in the Arctic with a top layer that remains frozen throughout the year

INDEX